Ruth Haag's

Management

Manifesto

Being a concise statement of the methods
needed to improve employee productivity

haag press

Ruth Haag's Management Manifesto

Text and Photograph Copyright © 2001 by Ruth S. Haag

Published by Haag Press 1064 N. Main St. #410 Bowling Green, OH 43402-1346
All rights reserved. No part of this book may be used or reproduced in any manner whatsoever without written permission except in the case of brief quotations embodied in critical articles and reviews.

Printed in the United States of America

ISBN 0-9710260-1-7

The biggest block to an employee's performance is their supervisor.

"Tell me about your favorite supervisor", Ruth asked her interviewee.

"They were like a mentor; they didn't micro-manage me. When I made mistakes they didn't get angry but helped me with the problems. I learned a lot, and enjoyed going to work."

"Tell me about your least favorite supervisor", Ruth then asked.

"They always intruded into work that I did. I could make no sense of what they wanted. They told me to do one thing, and then changed their mind and got angry. They made me work overtime but didn't pay me. I hated going to work."

Employees know what makes a good supervisor and what makes a bad supervisor. But when an employee becomes a supervisor, a transformation comes over them. Suddenly, they forget all of the things that they thought supervisors should do, and concentrate instead on what employees should do for them.

The employee says:

"If he wanted that, why didn't he just ask?"

While the supervisor says:

"Why doesn't he just know what I want?"

If supervisors could remember everything that they said and felt when they were employees, and unemotionally act on those memories, they would become excellent leaders.

A Story About a Typical Office

Joe arrived at work and went into his office. He wished that he had a window but he was not high enough in rank to deserve such a thing. He checked his E-mail, there were 20 messages. He sighed and started to read through them. Jerry leaned into Joe's office to say, "We're going to have a meeting about the Lewis contract, do you want to come?" Joe decided that a meeting sounded better than answering messages. Six hours later, the meeting adjourned without coming to any real conclusion. Joe got back to his office and started to look at the E-mail again. He got a telephone call from his son asking for help on a term paper. Paul came in and sat down and talked for an hour about various jobs, and some of his personal problems. Joe read a message from Donald, his supervisor, which stated, "As of today the office supply cabinets will be locked and the chief clerical assistant on each floor will have the key." Joe sighed again. He was sure that it would be next to impossible for him to get even a pencil. Joe had accomplished nothing with his workday. As he left for home, he took a portable computer for his son to use.

Donald, Joe's supervisor, did not know what to do with his employees. "People just don't have a good work ethic anymore", Donald complained.

An Analysis of this Typical Office

- The employees' physical working conditions depend on their level in the organization.
- Employees are productive less than 50% of the time.
- Meetings are long and pointless.
- Employees make personal use of company property without asking.
- Employees and supervisors are irritated and frustrated with one another most of the time.

A Story About an Unusual Office

Alex had to start early to go to work. He wanted to make lunch for the entire staff. He packed up his pots, pans, and food. He got into work at 7:30 AM. Since he arrived first, and it was going to be hot, he parked his car in the lot's shadiest spot, this time. At Alex's office there were no assigned work areas. He preferred to work at the conference table. Ben liked to sit on the couch. At about 8:15 the telephone began to ring. Within two minutes, four people called in from three different cities for the morning staff meeting. One of the callers was Alex's boss, Ruth, who ran the meeting. Ruth covered the plans and deadlines for the week. She introduced a new task and asked who wanted to do it. Tricia said that she would do it. The meeting was over in 20 minutes. When Ruth arrived at 12:25, most of the staff members were getting up from lunch. Ben spoke briefly with her about her weekend as she ate, and then went back to work. Tricia had to clear off the conference table for Ruth because Ruth had a meeting scheduled for 12:30 with another part of the staff. Later in the day Ruth checked on the staff members who were working in the office. They were pleased because their new computer database was working. Alex mentioned that he would be at the office the next day, rather than at home working; Ruth said fine. At the end of the day the staff was both frustrated and pleased by the new tasks they were working on, but had no real thoughts about the management of the company. Alex loaded up his pots and pans and headed for home at 6:00 PM.

An Analysis of this Unusual Office

- Physical working conditions are determined by the staff's needs.
- Employees are productive more than 90% of the time.
- Meetings are brief and to the point.
- Employees occasionally choose to use personal property to make their work go better.
- Each day ends with no irritation between supervisors and staff.

If these things happen, employees will be productive less than 50% of the time:

- **If there are annual evaluations and weekly edicts**

Most people spend about two weeks in irritation over their annual evaluation. During this time, they do almost no work. Most employees spend a day or two in irritation over restrictive edicts from supervisors, with the same work results.

- **If long pointless meetings consume employees' productive time**

Meetings are the best way to communicate information to the entire staff at one time. They are also a great way to discuss programs, with everyone who has input there at once. Meetings should last no more than an hour. Each meeting should have a specific goal and a specific conclusion. Anything else is a waste of time, and employees know it.

- **If employees are demeaned by an emphasis on the company's organizational chart**

Knowing where one fits in the organization is a good thing, but an emphasis on corporate hierarchy creates an unhealthy "class schism". Everyone should know who is in charge, but no one should be constantly reminded of their rank.

- **If employees must work for no pay**

Requiring overtime work and failing to pay for it is taking advantage of employees. The same is true of requiring them to incur out-of-pocket expenses on the company's behalf.

- **If there are incentive programs**

Incentive programs liken employees to pets who are given treats to perform. Having a program that demeans employees in this way is worse than having no program at all.

If the employee does a good job, they should be told. If they do a bad job, they should be advised about their problems. No certificates or candy bars are needed.

When these things happen, employees can be productive more than 75% of the time:

- **When managers enjoy being around employees**

When a supervisor thinks that the employees are less important and less intelligent, they then treat the employees that way. Employees are people with many strong points, as well as a few weak ones that have to be worked around.

- **When managers make the employees' work environment one where they feel comfortable and valuable**

Employees should not feel demeaned each time they reach their workstation. Postings on bulletin boards that essentially say, "You are a bad person" will demean them, as will office spaces that say, "You are a lesser person". The more that the workplace mimics a prison, the less productive the employees will be.

- **When managers make sure that the employees have the tools that they need to do their jobs**

Employees should not be frustrated by a lack of the supplies that they need to do their jobs. They don't need a luxury sedan if they are running errands, but they do need a vehicle that runs reliably. This same concept applies to their desks, chairs, and computers.

- **When managers make sure that the employees' personal items fit in the work environment**

Employees want their personal items to be well cared for while they are working. Everyone is sensitive about where they park their car, and where they keep their coat and lunch. The company needs to provide a system for these that is uniform. If one person gets a covered garage, all should.

- **When managers give employees controlled freedom**

As much as possible, each employee should determine their own work routine. Maybe the supervisor likes to do the hard tasks first and the easy ones later in the day, but what if the employee likes just the opposite? Everyone should be allowed to do tasks in the order that they want, as long as they get them done.

If the employee's job does not require specific arrival and departure times, then they should be allowed to choose their own schedule. If someone wants to come at 7:30 instead of 8:00 and leave at 4:30 instead of 5:00, what difference will it make?

- **When managers provide employees with predictable structure**

People work best if they know their limits. Work rules should be fair, clear, and consistent.

- **When managers follow the same rules as the employees**

If employees wear a uniform, then the supervisor should wear a uniform. If employees punch a time clock, then the supervisor should, too. When supervisors have the same work conditions as employees, they demonstrate that the rules are fair, and they have an easier time understanding employee problems and finding solutions.

- **When managers make sure that each employee is paid for all of the work that they do**

People like to be paid for the hours that they work. They like to be paid more if they work overtime.

- **When managers create an atmosphere where employees feel they belong**

The supervisor needs to create a feeling in the staff that they are all part of a group with the supervisor at the head.

The management system is not working if:

- Most days end with irritation on the part of the supervisor over what the staff has done, or has not done.
- The high turnover rate is explained by "People just aren't dedicated to their jobs."
- The staff is working productively less than 50% of the time.
- The staff is grumbling about the supervisor much of the time.
- The employees are stealing from the company.
- The supervisor says, "Every time I assign this, it fails."
- The supervisor spends a lot of time re-doing the staff's work.

The management system is working if:

- At the end of the day the supervisor looks around and says, "Wow, look at what they did."
- The supervisor likes to be with the staff at work.
- There is not a high turnover rate.
- The staff is working most of the time.
- There is no stealing from the company.
- The supervisor spends most of their time doing their own work.

If the supervisor can shift their focus from their own convenience, to their employees' needs, there is no end to what the employees will accomplish for them.

*With the exception of Ruth, Tricia, Alex and Ben, the names used in the stories are fictitious. This book is not intended to record historical fact.
Printed on 30% post-consumer recycled paper.*